SUCH A LIFE

SUCH A LIFE

Thelma T. Huber's Autobiography

A young woman's adventures as one of Goodyear's first "Crude Rubber People" and her fight for her family's survival as prisoners of the Japanese in the Philippines in WWII

Added materials by her son

Joseph C. Huber, Jr.

authorHOUSE®

AuthorHouse™
1663 Liberty Drive
Bloomington, IN 47403
www.authorhouse.com
Phone: 1-800-839-8640

© 2014 Joseph C. Huber, Jr. All rights reserved.

No part of this book may be reproduced, stored in a retrieval system, or transmitted by any means without the written permission of the author.

Published by AuthorHouse 11/12/2014

ISBN: 978-1-4969-3888-6 (sc)
ISBN: 978-1-4969-3889-3 (e)

Library of Congress Control Number: 2014919321

This book is printed on acid-free paper.

The life story of Thelma Belle Frances Thompson Huber
Edited and expanded by her son Joseph C. Huber, Jr.

Photo of Thelma as a twenty-two-year-old just
before she married and went to Sumatra

Preface

Thelma's is an extraordinary story of a young girl raised in a midsized Ohio town who found love and ended up traveling to the Far East where she spent a good portion of her life at a time when that part of the world was in turmoil. Adapting readily to strange environments and capturing the full spirit and joy of life, she helped her husband while he worked to develop a thirty-one-square-mile rubber plantation out of primeval jungle.

She was on the cutting edge of Goodyear's foray into rubber plantations in the 1920s and made a home, raised a family, and, with only a high school diploma, educated her children in the southern Philippines. As the wife of the plantation manager she handled all the social and management obligations that were entailed. When WWII and imprisonment by the Japanese came, she worked hand in glove with her husband to make a life for their family that was far better than that of virtually any others in the camps.

She met and charmed famous people and, until her death, maintained a worldwide correspondence. Her last years were spent in New Orleans, Louisiana, where she was visited in her home by many of the friends she had made in the Far East and elsewhere in her travels.

She had been around the world by boat, seeing the sights of Ceylon, Egypt, and Europe, had flown across the Pacific Ocean first class on the

Pan Am Clipper, and had made a home for her family on a few square feet of rough planking in the bottom of the cargo hold of a Japanese Maru freighter.

She was the granddaughter of Samuel C. Dyke, the man who invented the means to make inexpensive clay marbles and whose company, the American Marble and Toy Manufacturing Company of Akron, Ohio, started the business of selling toys to children. Merchants and ministers railed against this heresy, but the idea took off and made Akron the toy capital of the world until the Depression. Thelma's father's family descended from early settlers of Ohio, early enough to be considered among the first families of Ohio.

Divorces of parents and grandparents left her to make her way in the world on her own at an early age. When love came, she married her fiancé in haste just a week after she turned twenty-two, in time to go with him—a farm boy determined to do well—to an adventure in the jungles of Sumatra.

She rose to each challenge. In their biggest adventure, her skill, resourcefulness, and determination helped her and her husband cope with World War II and thirty-one months as prisoners of the Japanese in the Philippines. Their foresight, daring, and energy kept the family alive and well even in the hungry days at the end, which they estimated brought them to within two weeks of succumbing to starvation. The stress cost her husband and her years of their lives. Though civilians, they were recognized by order of Gen. MacArthur with campaign ribbons with a battle star.

Their travels and the many friends they made all over the world were important to Thelma. She had no known enemies. She successfully raised three children in extraordinary circumstances and she did a wonderful job of homeschooling them. Each of her children earned two college degrees from well-known universities.

Such a Life

During the preparation of this book, it was discovered that Thelma had some fascinating secrets. These are covered in Chapter 10.

Thelma Belle Frances Thompson Huber was born September 15, 1906, in Akron, Ohio; married September 22, 1928, in Akron, Ohio; and died October 6, 1973, in New Orleans, Louisiana. She is buried with her husband, Joseph Casper Huber, in the Rose Hill Cemetery on West Market Street, Akron, not far from the graves of her Dyke ancestors.

This far too brief account was dictated to a neighbor girl when my mother was not in good health and was mourning the loss of her husband. The only text changes were to correct the spelling and grammer of the scribe. Footnotes, inserts denoted by [ ] and ( ), and photographs have been added to provide context.

Joe Huber, Jr., August 2014

Image Acknowledgments

All images and photos are family items, with the following known exceptions:

- The map in Figure 5 is used by permission of the Goodyear Tire and Rubber Company; it appeared in the March 1945 issue of *Goodyear's Overseas News*.
- Figures 13 and 17 are used with the permission of the *Akron Beacon Journal*.

Table of Contents

1	The Early Years	1
2	Sumatra	8
3	Back in the United States	19
4	Pre-War Philippines	23
5	World War II	32
6	Manila – 1944-1945	38
7	Going Home	44
8	And Back to the Plantation	50
9	The Rest of the Story	52
10	Thelma's Secrets	58
11	Postscript	63

References 65

Chapter 1
The Early Years

I was born on the dining room table in the living room, probably screaming, as a table is not very soft. Father, Guy Thompson, worked nights, and after he came home that morning he had to sterilize everything before the Doctor came.

Figure 1: Thelma with her father, Guy Thompson, and mother, Grace Irene Dyke Thompson (later Hayes)

My Father's mother and father were English pioneers who settled in the middle of Ohio, so Dad was born on a farm. His parent had settled 160 acres. My Mother's mother, Belle, was from a French-English family, and her father, Samuel C. Dyke, was of German ancestry.[1] He was quite a man since he could speak, read and write seven languages. He also made the first marbles in the United State in 1890 in his porcelain factory in Akron.

When I was five, my brother, Ebert, and I had scarlet fever. We were quarantined with Mother, and Dad had to rent a room and stay outside for six weeks. He would knock on the kitchen window and ask Mother what she needed and then stick it against the kitchen door. Finally, liberation day! We sat on the front lawn while the house was fumigated. That was the year that Dad's father died of a heart attack on top of a hay wagon.

By the time I was eleven we had moved five times. I was spending most of the summers outside on the farm[2] with my Grandmother. That was fun as my only work was helping her with the chickens and ducks, churning butter and things like that. My uncle, Reason, who had taken over the running of the farm, taught me to ride horseback. Every Sunday my Grandmother and I got in the buggy and took off for church seven miles away. It was an all day excursion as we went to a relative's for lunch and finally ambled on home stopping at some other relative's for dinner.

---

[1] Samuel C. Dyke's biographer, Michael C. Cohill, writes that Samuel's parents came from Devonshire England just before our Civil War but does not state their ancestry.

[2] On the outskirts of Frazeysburg, Ohio.

Figure 2: Young Thelma on family farm near Frazeysburg, Ohio

It was just at this time that my parents were divorced and both immediately remarried: Mother to a Welshman (Joe Hayes), and Father to a young woman (Ella Young) who had lived next door to us, and who was a good friend of Mother. Father had custody of us two children until we were fourteen, and then we could choose.

By that time my Grandfather Dyke had moved his porcelain factory to Parkersburg, W. Va. My step-mother had had two boys and we had moved a couple more times.[3] My stepfather wanted to take Mother and me to Ireland to live, so I did go to live with them at fourteen; but not in Ireland.

So on to High School, as well as cramming in some business college. We were still on the move as we had moved two more times. I got a job as secretary at the Akron office of Prudential Life Insurance and, while working, took up dancing and banjo lessons in my spare time. I took ballet, exhibition tango and the Charleston.

I was 17, and still in school, when my Grandfather Dyke died. Since he and Grandmother were divorced, his estate went to his four children and seven grandchildren. He left his limousine to the Parkersburg Fire Department, and his wine cellar to a church. The church people wanted the wine delivered, so it got poured down the drain.

When I was nineteen, there was a lot of dissention at home between Joe Hayes and Mother, so I quit my job and went to Cincinnati for dancing engagements on riverboats and in private clubs. Then I went to St. Louis for more of the same and to model shoes for a large factory there. I went back to Akron at the end of summer and moved in with

---

[3] Note: Guy Thompson, Thelma's father, was adept at buying properties and improving them while the family lived there. He then sold them, purchasing another to repeat the process.

Dad and Ella. I got a job as private secretary to the manager of the Flying Squadron at Goodyear.

On my first day at work a handsome young man walked in. I poked the bookkeeper and asked who he was. She gave me his name and said he wasn't married. About a week later we had our first date and he immediately took me home to meet his family. About three weeks later we were going steady.

His name was Joseph C. Huber. His mother, Frances, had come from Munich.[4] His father, Louis, was from a small town outside of Munich.[5] They had lots of relatives in Ohio and Pennsylvania. Joe had 12 brothers and sisters, and when I met him two of them had died.

I had a 12-mile streetcar ride plus a long walk to get to work, so I rented a small, furnished apartment near the office, and hired a schoolgirl, whose mother was a widow, to keep it clean for me.

In the summer of 1928, Joe and I each had two-week vacations, and we took it at the same time. He and his brother, Bill, went to Lake Geneva. I went to Yellowstone National Park. On my first evening at a hotel in the Park I went for a walk through the trees. I came face to face with a large bear. He smelled me all over and then wandered off through the trees. The second day was nice – a bus ride around the canyons and on to a hotel.

After dinner I wandered down to the dance pavilion. The park hired college boys and girls to do the work in the summer, so there was plenty of dancing. The third day I was due at Old Faithful. I got there all right, but didn't see it as I was very ill. They sent for the ambulance and a nurse, and took me back to a small hospital near where I had been

---

[4] Burglauer—well north of Munich.

[5] Moosthenning—northeast of Munich.

that morning. The Doctor brought me out of my drugged state to tell me I had acute appendicitis and asked if I could pay for an operation.

I woke up the next morning in a large room by myself. The nurses used my room for a place to gossip, and the ambulance driver came in every day to sit on my bed and play cards. After two weeks he took me to the train and I headed for home. Actually, I had a five-week vacation and then went back to work.

September 1st, Joe came to my apartment and said he was leaving the next night for New York City and that I should have our banns published and he would return on the 21st and we would be married on the 22nd, so that is what I did. Our honeymoon lasted one night and then he went back to New York City.

Chapter 2

Sumatra

One week later, this man[6] came and whispered in my ear that if I wanted to see New York I had better quit my job and go right away. When I talked to the boss, he said he was expecting it but that I would have to train a new girl for a week, so we had three weeks in New York together. The beginning of the third week Joe called me and told me to go downtown and shop for clothes like mad. On Wednesday we went to Brooklyn and saw our ship leave.

We went to Akron for ten days, then on to San Francisco and caught the same ship. This was during Prohibition, but everyone on board seemed to have liquor except the Captain. Since we had the largest cabin[7], they all brought it to our cabin and the chief officer's servant would set up snacks, ice and the drinks and we all went there before dinner for drinks. We stopped in Honolulu and a priest came on board, on his way to Korea, and brought a large supply of drinks,

---

[6] From Goodyear.

[7] Goodyear's then First Class policy for company travel required first class accommodations.

which went in our cabin too. Then we went to Kobe and Yokohama in Japan, spending three days in each port.

Then on to Shanghai, Hong Kong, and Manila, making it to Singapore the day before Christmas. All of the Goodyear people came aboard and we spent the day and most the night with them. Christmas Day we went sightseeing and then had dinner with Swampy Marsh and family. That was amusing because his wife was upset with the servants because they had forgotten the potatoes. So after our coffee they put clean plates on the table and served the potatoes.

The next day, we went on to Penang, Indonesia, and spent the night there. The next morning at breakfast, the only other person in the dining rooms sat cat-a-corner from us. We thought he was complaining because the servants were all around him. Then we went out to the front veranda and he walked out and said "I'm Will Rogers, who are you?' My husband told him and then we sat up and talked for an hour and a half, and he told us what to see in Penang.

The next day we went to Medan, Sumatra where we were met by a Goodyear couple. Joe went shopping for a car and I went to buy dishes and glassware, 24 of each. That evening at cocktail time we met Heifetz and his wife. He had a concert that night in Medan.

We had to hire servants and the company would transport them for us to the plantation. A woman was to do the cooking and laundry, and her husband was to keep the house clean and serve our meals. The Company furnished a water carrier (a Tukeneyre), and a gardener.

After doing this, we went to the old plantation, Dolok Meranger. We arrived there on New Year's Eve, and slept at the guesthouse. However, I cannot say we slept because we had dinner with the couple that had met us in Medan. Then we went on to the head Dutch manager's house for fireworks that night. He used dynamite instead of regular fireworks, and blew out all of his windows. Then we had a midnight dinner with them.

We started out two days later in our new car with the American manager. We stopped for lunch in the jungle and sat on a log to eat food we had brought with us. Then we came to the first river. The only way to get across was to drive the car on a flat raft and we had to get out. It was muddy and I started to take my shoes off and the manager told me not to take them off. We arrived on the other side and had to go up a steep hill with a sharp turn in it. My husband gunned the car and we hit the side of the road, which knocked me against the windshield and then backed down on top my new hat, which I had bought in Singapore.

We finally arrived in a village that had a small hotel and stopped for coffee. I had to go to the bathroom so I whispered to my husband to ask the manager how to get there. This all had to be because we were just learning to speak Malay. The manager called a Malayan woman to take me to the bathroom, and she took me upstairs and gave me a baby's potty.

We went on from there, and because they didn't want our new car ruined crossing the next river they sent a company car with a Malay driver and a Filipino in it. I sat in the back with my feet up over the luggage, holding my birdcage with the canary that my husband had bought me in Hong Kong. My husband and the manager waded through the water and we made the other side.

We finally got to the rest house on Wingfoot Plantation, which was definitely jungle at that time. However, there was a small village and a few small shanties, which included the rest house and two old Japanese houses where the American manager and his assistant lived.

We spent the night at the rest house. There were two bedrooms and two baths, so-called. To take a bath one had to dump a pan of water over their body, which of course was cold. I got my dirty clothes off and opened the bathroom door, when a lizard hit me on the shoulder and took off down my back. I screamed, and even the manger came down to see what was wrong.

We had dinner that night with the manager and his wife, and the next day moved in to the new house the company had built for us. Later that day the manager's wife came over to show me how to put up mosquito netting around our bed.

Joe was in charge of the payroll and since Wingfoot plantation was 40,000 acres[8] and they were clearing the jungle, it meant a heavy amount of payroll. Joe and I would go down the river on the company boat to a town exactly opposite from Singapore, pick up the payroll, come back up the river and get on the little truck on the narrow gauge railroad and put the money in the office safe.

One trip, we got to the dock after dark and the truck had no lights. So Joe drove it and I hung over the side with a flashlight. Crossing our path was a huge gorilla monkey with a six-foot bunch of bananas under one arm.

We had our own small monkey who insisted that I bathe him every morning. He was fine until he got on the electric wires and got badly shocked. Joe rescued him and then he would have nothing more to do with Joe.

---

[8] I.e. 62.5 square miles.

Figure 3: Thelma and Joe in their Sumatra house

Our kitchen was very primitive in that it had a wood burning stove, and the oven had to be filled with wood until hot, then the wood pulled out and your cake put in, always hoping that your cake would get baked. I had to learn Malay in two months in order to speak to the cook and houseboy because they knew no English and some of the Dutch did not.

Since the cook did not know how to make fudge, I made it one day and the assistant manager's wife made it the next day. We played cards all morning and ate fudge and drank beer. My canary helped with the fudge.

One day I invited the Dutch women over for a party in the morning, when the houseboy came running in and said there was a python under the bathroom floor. I sent him running for help, and they tore up the bathroom floor and killed a twenty foot snake.

We had a very good Dutch doctor, and one night he called us to come and clean up the rest house so he could do an operation there. Afterwards we all stood and watched outside of the building.

The company had cleared enough jungle to make a new compound which included cement houses for all the American personnel, the two head Dutchmen, an Australian, a guest house, a hospital, and a nine-hole golf course, which was strictly for compound personnel only. Our windows were at a low level, screened and with shutters to close in case of rain.

One night while we were in bed a huge tiger came romping around outside the window. I jumped from my bed into Joe's and clung until the tiger got around the back of the house. It had already killed two men that night. The next day the men set up a trap and caught the tiger. Joe sent for me to bring our car and go and see the dead tiger. The Sultan of Bili had the choice of taking it or not, so he took it.

His son was a close friend of Joe and me and was educated in Oxford, England. He would drop in at night and we would have a drink and dinner together. When his father had had the tiger skin tanned, he had a large party for his friends and the American manager and wife were invited. Since we were friends of the son, we were invited too.

After a huge lunch and tour of the mansion, the son asked me if I would like to see the harem. When I said I would, he said that we had to take another woman along, so I asked the manager's wife to go. She agreed and he drove us there. His mother met us and served a big tea and we got to see all the young girls, because they peeked out of the rooms giggling to see two white women.

We went to the club one night and a burglar broke into our houses since the servants also had the night out. He found no money in our house because I had it well hidden, but he did find money in the next house. Joe was delegated to go up country and testify and also pick up the payroll there, so I went along and while he was in Court, I went to the market. I found some fresh corn and everyone got hysterical because I was testing the grains of it. They thought I was buying the worst corn.

We came back from there in our car with the payroll, and I sat with the forty-five on my lap all the way back.

On May 2, 1931, I woke up and told Joe that Grandma Thompson had died. He asked how I knew and all I could tell him was that I just did. Our mail took three months to arrive and Aunt Kathryn [Dad's youngest sister] wrote that Grandma had actually died that night.

It was the custom in the Orient for the men to come home for lunch and a nap. One day Joe had gone back to work when our little dog started barking frantically and the servants came in and found a snake in the dining room. They killed it so I could go back to my nap.

A short time later, Joe and I were reading at night, and he suggested we have a cold drink before bedtime. He called the houseboy, and when we got not answer he started out the swinging screen door. There were two steps down to the walk to the kitchen, garage and servants quarters. He went down the two steps and a six-foot cobra hissed at him, so he jumped back through the screen door. Then he yelled and told the houseboy to bring him a long stick by way of the front door, which he did. Joe went out with the stick and killed the cobra. The next day we had people coming to see it because the skin was beautiful.

A Dutchman went home on leave and Joe bought his Mynah bird as a gift for me. That thing woke us up at six o'clock every morning whistling the Dutch military tune. If Joe went out he would say, "Tabi, Tuan." If I went out he would say, "Tabi, Mem." So we would have to answer him.

Whenever one had guests in for dinner or lunch everything, according to the servants, had to be formal. There were eight Americans on the plantation for a couple of days, so I invited them to come for breakfast after a round of golf. I told them I would serve waffles. Then I had to explain to the houseboy about serving orange juice, having hot coffee ready, and to set up the waffle iron. I also had to explain to the cook how to make the batter for waffles. Try doing that in Malay. I could do it then but I can't do it now.

When the boy found it took so long for the waffles to cook, he went to the kitchen and came back to serve Joe a plate with three fried eggs and five strips of bacon, and a plate of toast. Then he stood in back of Joe and looked at me. When I smiled at him he went and served everyone the same thing. So our waffles when on, but just became a little treat.

It was Depression time, and Goodyear was sending some of its people home, but since they wanted Joe for the Pathfinder Plantation, they said that we could stay out our time. In January of 1932 we headed for home. Of course, at that time, it was only by boat, so we went to Penang and transferred to a round-the-world boat. When we got to Ceylon, a Goodyear couple met us, entertained us and took us shopping. We had saved an empty trunk, and so we bought five Oriental rugs and twenty-four ebony elephants and packed them the in empty trunk.

We went through the Red Sea, and when we got to Suez, we left all of our luggage on board the ship except for suitcases to give us a month in Europe. We hired a car to take us across the desert to Cairo, Egypt. As we started to get in the car an elderly woman and her son asked if they might go along. On the road there, we had to dodge Egyptians on leaping camels. It was very cold crossing the desert, and although I had a fur coat on, I finally asked Joe to let me sit beside the driver and have some protection from the wind.

The food in Cairo was terrific, also the service at the hotel. There were three bells on the wall, one for the housemaid, one for the houseboy, and the third for the Arab, so we had all the service we could use.

The day after arrival we called the Arab and went out to the pyramids. There we got on camels and rode them out to see the Sphinx.

Riding a camel is not easy since the camel goes down on his front knees and finally comes down behind; then you have to climb on and wrap your legs around his front hump, then you cling because he will try to bite you. We spent the rest of the day shopping in Cairo.

Figure 4: Thelma and Joe on camels by the pyramids

The next day we took the train and went to Alexandria in order to catch our boat again. We went across the Mediterranean to Naples. I have never been quite so seasick in my life. We had hired a travel agency to meet us and arrange transportation as needed and make hotel reservations. However, no tours. An Italian met us on the boat and we said we had two cartons of Camel cigarettes, and whom did we have to pay. He told us no-one because he would stick them in his pocket. He took us to the hotel and we spent about three day there, sightseeing and taking a trip to Bari. That was a beautiful place on a cliff where one could see the Adriatic Sea. We had planned to go to Sicily, but changed our minds because I had been so seasick.

We went by train from there to Rome and saw all the sights one should see including going to mass in the Cathedral, visiting the Coliseum, and going down into the Catacombs. We went on from there to Florence, arriving the Sunday before Lent. We strolled along the river and all the children were dressed in costumes but none of the parents were.

We had had breakfast in the hotel but we saw this gorgeous pastry shop so we went in there and ate another full breakfast. They brought everything in on trays and you helped yourself; then when you left they counted how much was gone and charged you for it.

We took the train from there to Venice, and on the train in the compartment were two Italian salesmen who wanted to talk, so with Joe's German, my French, and their Italian we made conversation. We spent about three days there and enjoyed it.

Then we went on to Milan and saw the picture of the Last Supper on the wall in a church. From there we took the train and after changing in Bern, Switzerland, we went to Interlaken for a three- day visit. When I arrived, the Swiss could not believe that I did not have boots, so they dragged out about twelve pairs until they could fit me. Interlaken is close to the Jungfrau Mountain with another mountain behind the hotel. Our beds were of deep feathers so that one sunk down in them, which, of course, kept one from getting cold.

The day we were to leave for Paris, the hotel fixed us a lunch to eat on our way to Bern. The train came in and then we couldn't find Joe, so the train waited while the whole hotel force went looking. He was in the village trying to find another little surprise for me.

We arrived in Paris, and since the company rules were that we had to travel first class, we had a lovely hotel. They served us hot chocolate and brioches in our room in the morning. Then we would bathe, get dressed, and go sightseeing.

We would go night-clubbing at night, and our most exciting evening was at the Follies Bergere, because Gloria Swanson and her husband sat in the same row with us. During intermission everyone went to the lobby and was served drinks. We took the train to go to the English Channel and since we had to take a boat across it and I was still remembering my last boat ride, Joe found me a room with a bath. I wasn't sick at all.

We arrived in Dover and took the train on to London. We were in London eight days trying to get a ship to New York. When we finally started to leave, we happened to see a Woolworth's store, so we put our luggage on board, kept the taxi and went back shopping. We bought the craziest things.

The trip across the Atlantic was rather dull as the ship could only carry twelve passengers and there weren't that many on board. The last 24 hours before we got to Manhattan we ran into a bad storm. The boat siren went constantly until we hit the river. This was in March of 1932. Our first night in town we were invited to have dinner with friends in Brooklyn. When we got out of the subway we were just two blocks from their apartment. However, we could not walk there because of the terrific wind, so we had to take a taxicab.

Chapter 3

Back in the United States

After a few days in New York we took the train for Ohio. We rented a nice apartment and then called the Customs Department to have our trunks delivered. The Customs man came with them and opened them in the basement. Joe and his brother, Henry carried things up as they were approved. When they got to the trunk with our ebony elephants in it, the customs man liked what he saw and said he would like one, so Joe gave him two. That was the end of customs.

We stayed in Akron, Ohio for a month. In that month Joe trained to be an adjuster of tires, so that it anyone got a defective tire, he could allow them so much on it. Then he was ordered to Philadelphia to take over that job there. We lived in a rented row house, and then I got rheumatic fever. He would carry me downstairs and put me on the couch and our next-door neighbor would come in and take care of me. The doctor finally told me that I needed my tonsils out. I became better after that.

Then in September of 1932 Joe was transferred to Miami, Florida, so after packing I went there too. Joe had to work long hours there, and so that I could have a way to get around he bought me a car with a rumble seat. [A Stutz Bearcat] We lived there a year and a half. In July of 1933, my brother in Ohio called and said we should do something for my mother and stepfather, since they had no money at all and were about to lose their house, so Joe told me to take the car and go to Ohio, take care of them and pay off the mortgage.

A friend of mine wanted to go along as far as Paris, Kentucky. When I picked her up she had her bulldog that she wanted to drop off in Georgia. While we were still in Florida, we ran into a heavy rain, and after passing two trucks the car skidded. She had been taking a nap and when I said "We're skidding," she grabbed the wheel. So we spun around about five times in front of the trucks and went over a six-foot bank into a swamp.

The car was on its side with her on the bottom, then the dog then me. All of the gasoline had leaked out into the car, so I reached up and turned the ignition off. By that time, the two truck drivers had stopped and were coming to rescue us.

The front truck had a colored driver, and when they had pulled us out of the window, the other driver asked if he was responsible for the accident. When I said no the colored man took off like mad, so the white driver drove us to the next town to a garage and we sent a tow truck back. We sat there and tried to get the gasoline off and the tadpoles out of our purses.

When the tow truck brought in the car, the police came along. They wanted the exact story and to know if we were hurt. They had come along the road and sat there guarding the car, which of course was filled with luggage. The garage put a new fender on it and a new tire and we took off for Georgia, because I didn't want Joe to worry. We just barely got into Georgia and stopped at an old-fashioned hotel. We walked about a half-mile up the railroad track to find a telephone so that I could call Joe. I did not tell him about the accident. Then we went back to the hotel and tried to wash the gasoline off of us in cold water.

We went on from there and when we got into Paris, Kentucky there were no signs so I stopped and asked a policeman if we were in Paris, because my friend wanted to catch a bus there. The policeman growled at us and didn't answer, so I went around the corner hoping to find the bus station. By the time I was one block away the policeman was by my side apologizing. He said that when he saw my Florida license he realized I wasn't just putting him on.

When I got to Akron, I rescued the parents and paid off the mortgage on the house, so they would have a place to live out their lives. Joe arrived a week later by plane and didn't even notice anything wrong with the car. Of course, I told him all about it at that point, since then he could not worry.

The morning of Dec. 24, 1933, now back in Florida, Joe called me and suggested I pick him up at noon, and we have lunch together. I did and we had lunch at a new place up the coast. Over our coffee he told me my Mother had died of cancer and he had made reservations on the train for me that night. His Christmas gift just happened to be a heavy coat. I spent Christmas day on the train, and since I was the only passenger on the train, the conductor suggested I use the stateroom instead of my bunk. It was 10 degrees below zero when she was buried.

After we got back to Miami I discovered I was pregnant, and seven months later Joe was transferred to New Orleans. We stopped for dinner on the way to the train and someone stole all of his clothes except his formals, which he left in the apartment. He arrived in New Orleans with no clothes at all.

The next day I started packing our trunks, then went to Hialeah to the horse races. I won on every race, so I thought that a good omen. About a week later I started for New Orleans in the car, and he had not yet found an apartment. I went looking and found one at the corner of

St. Charles and Napoleon. I told the landlady that I was going to have a baby, and she said "Obviously."

So after guests from Sumatra and deciding on names, Joe, Jr. was born at Baptist Hospital. He tried to come down feet first. I was in the hospital for two weeks, and then the doctor recommended that I go to Abita Springs for two weeks and completely relax. Then I came home and we moved into a double shotgun house in Lakeview. I had just hired a new maid when we had our notice to leave for the Philippines.

We left New Orleans when Joe Jr. was seven months old. I had to take him downtown one day to see about our passports, and shots, and since it was so hot I didn't have any shoes or socks on him. Some women passed me on St. Charles Street and told me that that was no way to treat a baby. We went to Akron for about ten days and stayed with Joe's people, and then we were on our way.

Chapter 4

Pre-War Philippines

Our trip to the Philippines was very nice. Not only was it fairly smooth, but there were three or four couples on board who were going to Java to open a new plant for Goodyear. Also, there was a nurse who fixed Joe Jr.'s formulas and brought them to the room. If we were busy she would feed him. Joe washed his clothes and hung them in our bathroom as it took the ship's laundry three days to do them and we didn't have that many things.

Whenever we reached a port, the nurse spent most of her time with Joe, Jr. so we could go shopping.

We had to change boats in Manila. When we arrived in Zamboanga, Goodyear's troubleshooter met us there and introduced us to all the white people and the merchants. Shortly after dinner we got on the company's launch[9] and started our 14-hour trip to the plantation[10]. Our transportation from the dock to the office was a flat car [with seats] drawn by a carabao on narrow gauge rail tracks through the mangrove swamp.

---

[9]   The launch Pathfinder Estates.

[10] Pathfinder Plantation.

We went to the house and breakfast was ready. There were servants hired except for an amah for Joe, Jr. That only took a matter of minutes. The troubleshooter stayed for two days and then left for the States. There was a Swiss assistant on the plantation so it didn't take long to get settled in. When we went to town, which was about every three months, we took a servant along so I was free to roam the shops.

Pathfinder Plantation is ~2,500 acres. It is surrounded on one side by a river[11] and the rest of the way by hills and jungles. When we arrived in 1935 most of the trees were ready for tapping.

---

[11] The Kabasalan River.

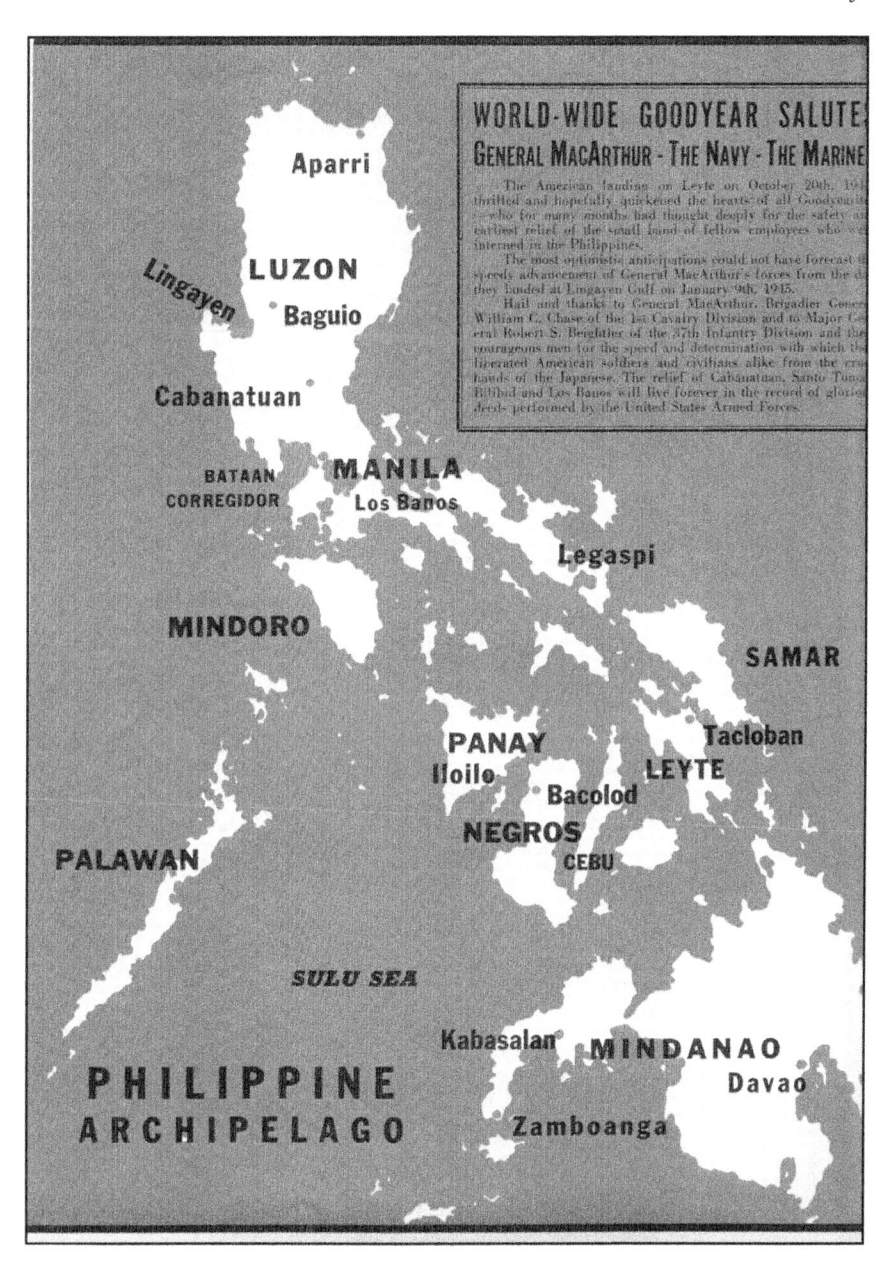

Figure 5: Map of the Philippines showing Kabasalan,
the location of the Wingfoot Plantation

On April 1, Goodyear sent a couple to stay with us for about three months to get a shipment of young trees [rubber seedlings] ready to go to Costa Rico and to go with them to protect them. I was so sick the day we left the plantation that I could hardly pack. On the way to the dock I slid off the flat car and took all the skin off my spine. I went to the hospital and found out I had malaria and was pregnant. The baby was due sometime in December, and I was advised to come and stay in town from the 1st of December. Barbara was born early on the morning of Dec. 31st [1935] with no fuss. We went to the plantation a couple of weeks later.

Figure 6: Joe in front of the 13,000 square-foot Manager's House

In September of 1936, I decided I must be pregnant again. So I went to town and the doctor said, definitely, but he couldn't tell when. He suggested I come to town the middle of November and stay there. Stephen was born on December 17th so I was still in the hospital for Christmas. When I had been there two weeks I suggested to the doctor that I move to the hotel and hire a nurse. His idea was that I stay there and do my running around and the nurses would take care of Stephen. I was in town a month before Joe could come after me.

At Christmas time it was the custom for the office employees and wives to come caroling, send a pig to be barbecued, and bring an orchestra. We were expected to furnish the rest of the food and drinks and have a room ready for dancing. We went along with it and it was always a pleasant evening.

In 1938 two couples that came to visit were on their honeymoons. Sounds like a funny place for a honeymoon – in someone else's house!

The houseboy woke Joe early one morning to say there was a snake in the chicken coop, so he went out to shoot it. This was all in 1938 and we had our thoughts on our trip home in 1940.

Figure 7: Thelma's three children—from left, Joe Jr., Stephen Louis, and Barbara Jean

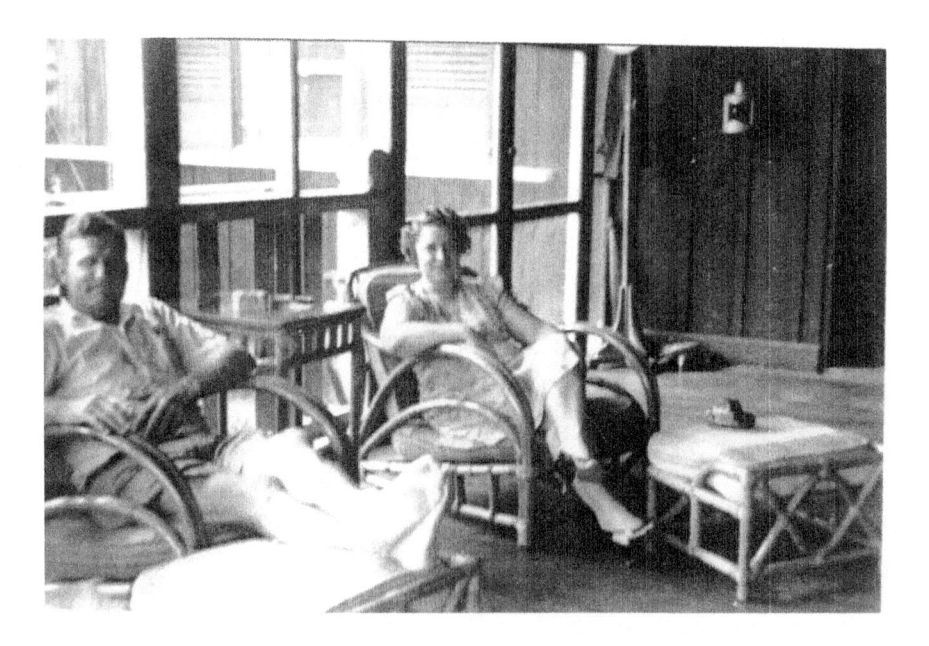

Figure 8: Thelma and her husband, Joe, on the porch of the prewar house

It was the custom to pack everything one owned and take it with them. So we spent most of February doing this and left at the end of the month. Our trip across the Pacific was on a luxurious liner, the President Coolidge. They even had a dining room for the children, and meals were served at different times. In Shanghai, we ordered a complete set of luggage to be made of blond calf to be ready for us when we returned in six months, even down to a cosmetic bag.

We spent three months with Joe's people, and then rented a house for two months. The last month we rented a cottage on a lake, so it was an ideal place to do our packing. We left the 1st of October to go back to the Philippines. Our trip to the Coast was fun. On our way to Hawaii, a Chinaman was found hung in the bedroom. He had had $5,000 stolen from him – his life savings. The police held up the ship to investigate and finally his body was locked in a broom closet. There was a big fight of the dock than night before we sailed.

We were part way across the North Pacific when the weather got really rough. The Captain announced that we would have to pass directly through a typhoon, as there was no way to bypass it. The ship went to a 42-degree angle, portholes were shattering and furniture was breaking loose. One of our trunks went through the bedroom door. Joe put the children under a couch for protection. Finally, the crew made a lifeline and got us all to the top deck [the lounge], where we all laid on the deck. The next morning the weather had calmed down so the crew could start repairs, like putting the piano up a deck and cleaning the ketchup out of the new cars.

Figure 9: The lounge of President Coolidge in the typhoon of 1940. Barbara and Joe Jr. are sitting up while Stephen and Thelma are lying down.

When we reached Kobe, Japan, one of the crewmen was out over the deck when he fell onto the dock. It seemed to be a bad luck trip. Really, the only good thing was arriving in Shanghai and finding our luggage waiting for us.

When we arrived in Manila, of course we had to change boats, so we stayed at the Manila Hotel for a couple of days. We were on the 5th floor. The morning after we arrived the whole staff went on strike. We had to walk up and down the stairs and go out for meals. I went out shopping in a cab one day. We were in the second lane of traffic when an American woman ran in front of our car. We didn't hit her but the next car did. When we left to catch our boat we had to carry all of our luggage downstairs. Pathfinder looked so good.

Then came 1941 and turmoil. The Army and Navy wives were ordered home. The Assistant's wife decided to go as they had a small baby. I decided that the children and I would stick it out with Joe. We had a high-powered radio that could get Tokyo, San Francisco and England so we really know what was going on. By that time I was teaching the children from the Baltimore Correspondence School[12], Joe, Jr. in the first grade and Barbara and Steve in Kindergarten. Joe, Jr. loved it all so much that he took that too. By the middle of the year we started on the 2nd year of school. Things were very tense, of course.

---

[12] Calvert Home Instruction.

Chapter 5

World War II

When Pearl Harbor came [Dec. 8, our date] Joe was due to go to Zamboanga. He had had an air-raid shelter built under one bedroom. He warned us if any planes came over, we should go to the shelter. The houses and village were completely blacked out.

The first two planes we got under the shelter for, the third we all crawled in one bed because we were tired of the mosquitoes. The first two, as we found out later, were Japanese and the third was an American trying to escape Manila. He didn't, as he came down in Zamboanga. On Joe's trip he bought $1,000 worth of canned goods, got all our money and the company's he could out of the bank. Our launch was in dry dock at this time so we couldn't run for Australia. Joe decided to get rid of the Moros on the plantation, as there were unpredictable. Then he kept the regular force working until the end of the year and gave the regular employees ground to build gardens on.

Shortly after that, two Filipino men brought a white man up my back steps and dumped him. I had never seen him before, and he was exhausted. I managed to get some water down him and dragged him into a bedroom until the cook and houseboy arrived to take care of him.

Such a Life

Our next guests were an elderly couple, their daughter and her two young children, then an English remittance man[13] and a couple about our age. Also, they brought our launch along. The Filipino/American guerila army heard about it fast and came down through the jungle to requisition it and part of our canned food. Joe moved the elderly couple, family and their friend and the remittance man to the Assistant's house as the assistant had taken off by foot for Zamboanga.[14] We bought two cows with calves so we would have plenty of milk for all and be able to save the canned milk.

Before our guests arrived, we went up into the hills to our hideout there, near the Subanos. They were friendly and loved watching me wash clothes in the river. We had a murderer come up through the jungle every day with fresh bread and ice. The Filipinos had released him from jail when the Japanese started taking over. He had come back to his native village, Kabasalan, which was next to the plantation.

After three weeks there we decided we might as well be comfortable and at home and have more food. We went back to the house and nothing had been touched, but the animals had been fed and cared for. We figured if the Japanese came in fighting we could run to the hills day or night as we had the place well stocked with everything.

As it happened they came the night of June 30th. A Filipino came running to tell us they were at the dock, so we had the houseboy run out and hide the radio. When the Japs arrived at the plantation, they ran our guests out of the assistant's house, not even giving them time to collect their things, so we had a houseful again.

The Jap Commandant sent for Joe, so he went prepared with the safe and record keys. They had a formal meeting and Joe was told

---

[13] Someone paid by his family to live in a foreign country to avoid family embarrassment.

[14] Half of the way was through primeval jungle without a road.

through the interpreter that we would leave Kabasalan on the morning of July 3rd, taking only what we could carry. The Commandant and the interpreter (who had been our photographer) wanted to see the house. I showed them around formally and then I was told we could take anything we liked. The Japs seemed to enjoy dropping in and just sitting around.

The houseboy and I started cooking things to take along. We made a huge beef roast and someone brought us a large sack of sweet potatoes, so that turned out to be July 4th dinner for thirty-nine of us.[15] When we got to the river on the 3rd of July, there were 3 Japanese boats: a large one that took off, a launch that took us and a high-powered launch that could chase us around. I was asked if I had any pencils or paper and I had to say yes, and that I had schoolbooks. They took these away for inspection then returned them to me.

After dark we walked into a friend's house where there were already twenty-five people: our first concentration camp. We had to sleep on the floor, but I can't say the Japs were bad. They took a marketing tour out every morning, and although we were spending our own money we had enough to eat, although not too varied. The women took turns doing the cooking each day with two men to help them. I had told the interpreter that I needed to go to the dentist, so a guard came every morning for several mornings and the Dentist would slip me money for one of the women in camp.

After six weeks of that we were told to pack and were taken to a Jap ship and put in the hold. A couple of days later we arrived in Davao and were taken to a convent.[16] We scrambled around looking for a spot for

---

[15] At the Zamboanga Concentration Camp where others had already been gathered. There were thirty-six, not thirty-nine of us.

[16] Del Pilar Convent School in Davao.

the 5 of us to sleep. The American interpreter walked out of a private bedroom and offered it to us as she had received a better room. The whole place was filthy, as Jap soldiers had been living there. In the next day or so, one hundred and seventy-two people were brought in from the Lake Lanao section.

We kept up our separate cooking areas and messes. In the time we were there, I got the flu and a Jap guard with a bayonet escorted four men with me on a door to the hospital. The Filipino doctor was very good and the first thing she gave me was a glass of milk. Also, Barbara fell out of a tree into a large pan of roasting coffee beans. Instead of crying she just headed for the building. The Japs sent a guard with my husband Joe and Barbara to the hospital for treatment.

Then we moved to a cabaret [The Happy Life Blues 3.8 km. south out of town on the South Road]. We were allotted so many square feet of floor space[17] for each one.

The Japs brought in about 60 more people, missionaries from Eastern Zamboanga. Things were very primitive as we had to go to the bathroom by squatting behind two pieces of tin, until the men could make a wooden commode. To take a bath, the Japs would turn on one spigot for an hour so at least 6 of us would have to crowd together and wash.

The [Episcopal] priest in camp took over the cooking and I was in charge of a vegetable cleaning crew. This gave me time to get on with the children's schoolwork. Joe was in charge of a wood cutting crew to keep the fires going.

He had talked the Japs into giving us some ground so we could build a shanty. Every day he would drag home a piece of bamboo and

---

[17] Four feet by seven feet, or twenty-eight square feet.

then in the afternoon he would talk a guard into taking him and the children out for cocoanut fronds, from which we wove siding and a roof.

The house consisted of a large bedroom, on the second floor, with the bed about 1½ feet up, two windows and shelves for the few clothes we had. The lower floor was a dining room and kitchen with an open burner stove and hand washbasin. Under the bedroom was a large sitting room and we had a lawn out to the fence. The whole house was made with one nail.

Figure 10: The family's shack at the Happy Life Blues Internment Camp south of Davao on Mindanao

At that time, Filipino wagons would come by and the Japs would allow us to buy coconuts and raw peanuts if we had money. Joe built me a coconut grater so I started in the oil business. It meant grating the coconuts, then boiling them for 5 hours. The oil was fine for cooking and there was a brown residue that the old men like to eat with their rice, so they came and stood in line for it.

Figure 11: The Coconut Oil Factory under the family's shack

Chapter 6
Manila – 1944-1945

We were there until Christmas Eve of 1943, when we were ordered on a Jap boat. We were so crowded we had to sleep end to end. We left the next day from Manila. It took us till January 2nd to arrive there. We were taken to Santo Tomas, which was the University. It was large but there were 4,000 of us there, plus the Jap guards.

Every able-bodied person had to work, so I got a job as private secretary to the American Chief of Police and Joe was put in charge of a carpenter crew. Joe bought some land with a primitive shack and built a nice shanty with wood floors. The food ration kept getting worse and worse. We were all losing weight like mad. By the end of 1944 it consisted of a half cup of uncooked rice per day.

Figure 12: The Family's shack at Santo Tomas

In September, the Americans started bombing Manila. They know our location so did not bomb there but we occasionally got pieces of shrapnel. In fact, one night just as we stood up to go to bed a large piece came down through my chair. Joe had carved a wood gun with a bayonet on it for Steve. The Japs happened to see it at roll call one morning. After thoroughly examining it, they announced over the loudspeaker that there must be no more made.

The bombing increased so it was a day and night deal. We were, of course, not allowed to have a light of any kind. For something to do at night, we all took turns saying the multiplication and division tables. I'm sure the children will never forget them.

For Christmas that year, a friend of mine suggested we make a fruitcake. She had cassava flour, 2 preserved eggs and some other little thing. If I would just donate the 3 bananas the children were getting (a special treat) and furnish the fire, we could make and share it together. Then the question was to find a one-pound coffee can to bake it in. Surprisingly, it turned out well.

One night early in February 1945[18] there was a loud crash and shooting in the camp. We ran out of the shanty to the road to see what was going on. A Jap thrust his bayonet at us and ordered us back. It was two American tanks and a car. They killed the Jap Commandant, which didn't quite make up for the four executives of the camp that he had slaughtered. The Jap soldiers huddled up in the Education Building, which was directly across from us. The Americans left a tank in front of the Main Building and the other tank came down to the Education building [cattycorner across the road from us]. The car backed up against our shanty and shortly afterward the leader of the Americans was injured. People kept creeping into our shanty from the back to see what was going on.

Daylight came and the Japs started sniping. The leader of the Americans decided that he would let the Japs go in order to rescue all the Americans in that building, so the next morning they were escorted out and taken some distance away. Manila and surrounding country was still held by the Japs. The tanks and jeeps[19] had come through the Jap camps and they just stood and stared.

---

[18] February 3.

[19] The 700 member Flying Column of the First Cavalry with elements of the 44th Tank Battalion.

The shelling of the camp by the Japs started then. We were in our air raid shelter one day and two American soldiers were just outside the entrance. One wished for a cigarette so Joe dug out a pack we were hoarding. I thought they would both die coughing.

Another time they had located our row of shanties. They [Japanese artillery] were blowing up every other one. The second from ours came down on their roof and we were hoping the next one would be a little defective. Just then the shelling stopped. Evidently the Americans had located the mortar.

The worst night was when we were ordered to evacuate our section and go and lie behind the Education Building. The Japs were shelling our area and the Education Bldg. We went and lay in the rain. The shells were breaking over our heads. Joe touched me and said he was sick and would I try and get a doctor. I went into the building and was ordered out as they were giving a transfusion. I got back to the door and a soldier asked if he could help.

We wound our way through the shanties and found the doctor. He went with me to where Joe should have been, but he had gone to the shanty. The doctor and I went over and he gave me a slip to get him some extra food in the morning. The night went on with going to the children and then to Joe.

When I was at the shanty once, the Japs blew a big hole in the road [path] I was traveling. At daybreak, the shelling stopped and I went for Joe's extra food, which turned out to be a good thick soup.

Joe, Jr. and Barbara made all the UP papers in the States. They were sitting on the gun of one of the tanks with another boy when the UP photographer took their picture. When the families and friends in the States saw them it was the first news they had that any of us were alive.

Figure 13: Thelma's father, Guy Thompson, looking at picture of Joe Jr. and Barbara on a tank as seen in Akron Beacon Journal of February 16, 1945.

Figure 14: Our family after rescue—down to skin and bones

Chapter 7

Going Home

In March, the Americans had taken over Manila except for a few scattered snipers. They started trying to get us out. The first plane to go had the nurses who had been at Corregidor and Bataan. One poor girl had had her nose blown off.[20]

It came our turn to go and we were loaded into a truck and taken on a tour of the blown up city. One plane had taken off when we arrived and we had to wait until it got to Leyte. They ran into bad weather and it was too late for us to leave, so we were taken back to camp. We started again the next day after the Red Cross had given Joe and me each $25.00 for spending money. On what?

We got into our Mae Wests (a life jacket in case we were shot down over water). The plane zigzagged around the field because of all the shell holes. We got over the rim of the mountain and one of the crew came and asked if our children could go up in the cockpit with them.

---

[20] She had been with us for a few days in Davao, one of ten on a seaplane trying to escape from Bataan. Per "We Band of Angels' her nose had been injured in a crash landing before their capture on Mindanao.

The Japanese shot at us from small islands with anti-aircraft guns. Fortunately, they missed and we got to Leyte. What a shock, as they ordered the women and children into one truck and the men into another. Joe was taken to a dispatch camp and the rest of us to a hut surrounded by disabled soldiers. I had never seen so many able men as when we drove up. Two days later Joe managed to hitch hike a ride to our camp to get his razor and a change of clothes. The Navy started coming over to ask permission for our children to go aboard for lunch. They enjoyed it and I am sure the Navy men did.

Figure 15: A group of the children talking to the ventriloquist dummy on Leyte. Stephen is the blond on the right. Barbara is half hidden behind him, and Joe Jr. is the closest to the dummy wearing an army cap.

We were there 10 days and then put aboard a ship. I chewed my nails all night about Joe, but at daylight the men were on the dock.

We couldn't sleep on the same deck or have our meals together, but we could see each other. We were only served two good meals but the waiter brought in extra bread and meat at breakfast and suggested we make sandwiches.

We went by convoy to Biak, Borneo which was bombed the night before we arrived and the first night we were there. Then on to Hollandia, New Guinea, and then Finschaven. The Red Cross met us there with army clothes. The children's things were quite big but we managed across the Pacific. The convoy broke up in Finschaven, and we zigzagged across the Pacific because of Jap submarines. We had to go on deck every morning and evening in our Mae West's as that was the most likely time for the Japs to attack us.

The Golden Gate never looked so good as it did on that April 21, 1945. My aunt, some of our friends and two Goodyear men were there to meet us. They had a hotel suite arranged for us, money, and the option of leaving for Ohio that night or waiting two weeks. We decided to leave. We went to the hotel and the friends wanted to take the children and me shopping. I said that if they didn't mind I wanted to sit in the tub until lunchtime.

**Figure 16: Our welcome at San Francisco –
Left to right, back row—Thelma's aunt Ethyl Dyke, Thelma, Ethyl's friends Hazel Batchelor and Ethyl Batchelor, Miriam Barnes (another of Mom's relatives), and Joe Huber.
Left to right, front row—Stephen, Joe Jr., and Barbara on the dock at San Francisco, arriving from the Philippines.**

So they took the children and bought them whole new outfits, which included underwear from under the counter after my friends told them how much there were needed. Barbara was given a large doll, the boys toy guns, and they even bought me two dresses and gave me a very good coat, so, I could go to Ohio, even in white shoes.

We left on the train that evening. It was really crowded and we had to stand in line to get dinner. When we arrived in Akron, the family and friends were there as well as the Press. The company had a large suite in the best hotel reserved for us. The Press kept crowding around so we got a lot of pictures out of it. After six weeks the children were getting restless and Joe suggested I call his mother and we go there and stay until we could find a house to buy. That is the only time she sounded angry at me and her reply was "I thought you were <u>never</u> coming."

Figure 17: Safely back and with normal clothes at the Akron Mayflower Hotel after thirty-one months as prisoners and survivors of the thirty-day Battle of Manila that saw 120,000 killed.

Such a Life

We bought a house, completely furnished, on a fresh water lake. It was a three story building and had a dock and a good swimming place. On Saturday, it got to be a habit for me to put a large turkey in the oven and go and do Joe's mother's shopping. By the time we got home some of the family was there. We never seemed to have any turkey on Monday.

[What Thelma does not mention is the fact that she and her husband were each, by command of General MacArthur, awarded the Asiatic Pacific Campaign ribbon with one battle star and the citation below. This must make her among a very small group of women to earn a combat ribbon with a battle star, as a civilian prisoner.]

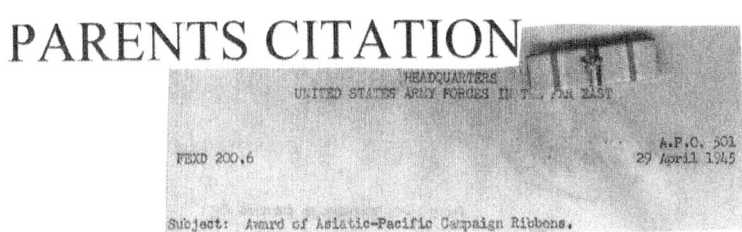

PARENTS CITATION

HEADQUARTERS
UNITED STATES ARMY FORCES IN T... FAR EAST

FEXD 200.6

A.P.O. 501
29 April 1945

Subject: Award of Asiatic-Pacific Campaign Ribbons.

Joseph C. Huber Sr. and Thelma T Huber - - - have by their fortitude and courage, contributed materially to the success of the Philippine Campaign.

By Command of General MacArthur

Figure 18: Their combat ribbons

Chapter 8

And Back to the Plantation

Joe headed back for the Philippines in November, 1945. Women and children weren't allowed then. He went on a ship that had 4 men passengers and they had to sleep in little cabins on the poop deck. I had all the children's tonsils taken out about Easter. Then they got chicken pox. We had to have inoculation and when the Doctor heard that he came to the house with our shots.

The children and I we were on the first boat out allowed to take women and children. It was like old home week, as we knew so many people on board. One day some of us were talking in the lounge when a woman ran in screaming, "Come see your children." I headed for the deck and started running. When I could see them, I made myself cool it and strolled on. They were all on a beam out over the Pacific. I told them it was time to come down and they did. Then I had to explain that that was no place to be.

When we got to Shanghai we got a launch and went ashore. We walked to our favorite hotel and had cokes. We had planned to shop but the Chinese were glaring at us so much that we went back to the ship. Hong Kong was fine.

When we got to Manila, I think every white man in town was on the dock. A Filipino friend was there, too, and got me through customs with a wave of his hand. The Goodyear men took the children and entertained them so Joe and I could have some time alone.

We flew to Zamboanga. When we got partway a storm had closed off our route so we went miles out of our way. We came down one place in a pouring rain and only stayed there a few minutes. It was dark when we approached the Zamboanga airstrip so one of Joe's friends had come out with his jeep [to mark the runway with its headlights]. We made it down safely.

When we got to the Plantation the next morning, breakfast was ready the way I like my eggs. After that the servants came in to say hello. Since our big house had been accidentally burned by the guerrillas, funny, they apologized to me, we were living in a smaller one and so only needed the cook, houseboy, laundress and gardener. The children were much too old for amahs.

By this time we could take the houseboy with us on our trips instead of amahs. The kids all loved the movies and buying fruit to eat during them.

We had the usual visitors and had a funny monkey for a pet. One night to entertain some friends, we had a cookout. Suddenly the monkey was on the table helping himself. We started roasting marshmallows and he sat on a rock beside me and would pull my stick over and eat my marshmallows. He had his own pet – a small pig. He would feed it some of his rice and then go and sit on it and scratch. That seemed to be the year for wild animals.

Chapter 9

The Rest of the Story

We got swinging on the schoolwork. Barbara and Stephen were almost finished with grammar school, and Joe Jr. his first year of high school when the company invited us to come to Akron, Ohio for the 50th anniversary of Goodyear. On the only boat we could get out we were the only passengers but one. We went south to get around the lower end of Luzon. The ship was on standby for a couple of days because there was a volcano erupting and they might have to rescue people. We had two days and a night with a friend on the Del Monte plantation.

When the all clear came, we went up the coast and they loaded mahogany logs on the deck. This made for a rough trip across the Pacific, and the way the boat rolled we weren't sure we would make it. The ship, the Christer Salen, did break in half six months later. We did manage to finish the schoolwork.

Figure 19: The Crister Salen with heavy logs on deck

We got to Akron in October, and when we had a free moment we went to talk to Joe's mother. We asked how she would feel if the children stayed with her. She acted delighted as it meant people in the house who could go shopping. We told her we would take over the bills and what did she think if we could talk her widowed sister into coming there to live with a salary and who would be a help to her. That was wonderful. There were five bedrooms so that was no problem.

Joe took the children to register them in school. They screamed over their ages and I got upset when the children came home all put back a grade just to try to hit their age brackets. Those rough miles on the Christer Salen!

We left in February 1949. Joe felt he should go back for another 3 years and train a man for his job. Our trip out was nothing to write home about – about 9 passengers. After we got there I went on a sewing spree and made Barbara a lot of dresses. I knew her measurement so that she could put on a dress and wear it the day she got it.

In June of 1951 Joe came tearing up to the house with a cable in his hand. The company suggested that because of the Korean War, I and the assistant's wife and two young sons should come home. We both thought they should go and there was no way to send them if I didn't go, so Joe cabled that we would be on a certain boat a month later. They cabled back "suggest you put them on a plane as soon as possible." We packed frantically, then Joe sent the Assistant to Manila with us so they would have longer together.

There was a big party for us in Zamboanga. Our pilot for the next day told me to make him stop drinking at 12:00. I tried but it was 2:00 AM before his wife and I dumped him in bed. We took off the next morning and he waved at me to come up. When I got there, were almost over the plantation, close enough for me to see everyone's face. Joe looked shocked as were way off course and if we had had trouble we were really in it. It was mountainous directly ahead and unexplored country.

We made it to Manila and there were parties there for us. One of the men told me if we lost one engine not to worry; two, I should worry a little about it: three, really worry and the fourth, get ready for a nosedive. After a couple of days our plane took off at midnight. Talk about red carpet treatment. We had the first four seats in the plane and the crew and pilots gave us their section with eight seats.

We went by way of Guam, Midway, Wake and Honolulu. The stewardess made up beds for us like huge Pullman beds. I slept so hard she had to shake my arm to offer me a cup of coffee before we landed in Honolulu, and I barely got it down.

We had to go through customs there rather than at San Francisco. I had to open one of my bags and I was through. The Assistant's wife had to open all of hers. When she was finished we went into the dining room for breakfast. The loud speaker came on and she and I were asked to come to the customs counter in the lobby. When we go got there we were asked to dump out our purses. The contents were OKed so we finished our breakfast and got on the plane. I was relieved of the orchid I was wearing which a friend in Hawaii sent me.

Six months later the assistant's wife and I were invited to a luncheon. She walked in with a bouquet of flowers for me. I gasped and said, "But these are from the Philippines." She said she had smuggled in the bulbs and grown them in her bathroom window. So that explained what had happened in Honolulu.

When we got on board she and the children had been moved to the back of the plane. I was still in the crew's quarters with the airline doctor and a very austere lady from Australia. As we got off the ground the Captain came back and asked my name. When I told him he invited me up to ride in his seat. He introduced me to the navigator and co-pilot. There was a gorgeous view of the Hawaiian Island and the ships plodding along below us.

There was a deck below us with a lounge and bar, so the Assistant's wife and I spent most of the trip there together. We went back to our seats for dinner and then it got so rough they couldn't bring us coffee.

When we arrived in San Francisco, Goodyear had a suite reserved for us at a hotel, and two Goodyear men met us to take us there. She and the boys left the next night by train and I went to visit my aunt in Berkeley and friends down the Coast. I arrived in Akron on Valentine's Day. Joe's mother was especially happy when I bought a sedan right away and we could all go to church together. Also, there was someone to take care of their finances, go grocery shopping and take the aunt to her card games.

Joe came home in April of 1952 and I met him in San Francisco. He had a real pearl bracelet for me, given to him by a Chinese friend of ours. He made it home in time for Joe, Jr's high school graduation at which he was valedictorian. Joe, Jr's science project for graduation was an electronic organ.

Joe Jr. took some kind of college entrance exam and was offered scholarships at Carnegie Tech, Princeton, Yale and M.I.T. It took him two weeks to decide that he wanted M.I.T. He went up to Cambridge, Massachusetts by himself and two weeks later I was invited with other mothers of new students to a tea. Joe sent me up and suggested I spend a few days and see Boston. Joe, Jr. went through the school years and stayed to get his Masters.

Joe took his 6 month vacation and when the company realized he meant he wasn't going back to the Orient they offered him a new job as rubber inspector and exporter/importer. They suggested New York City, New Orleans or Mobile. New York was out as far as we were concerned and he settled on New Orleans. He had to go to New York for a couple of months to get acquainted with his job. He invited me up for a weekend as he had in mind buying me a fur coat and wanted to see them tried on.

Joe left for New Orleans Dec. 26, 1952. He spent the next three or four weeks getting his office set up. The company had rented a two room office in a bank building and sent the furniture down from Akron, including a teletype. He had to hire a secretary and look for a house. He found the bottom floor of a new duplex and managed to get a stove and ice box installed. Barbara, Steve and I drove down during the Jan. school break. Joe had them registered at Newman School. Barbara and I had to go back to Akron for her graduation in June,

We stayed in the duplex until 1957. In the meantime, Barbara had married [Robert Hall] her Professor in Fine Arts at Newcomb [Sophie

Newcomb College of Tulane University]. Steve had gone to LSU and decided to get his service duties out of the way before finishing college. So he joined the Air Force for four years. Our landlord came one day and asked us to move upstairs so his son could have the downstairs. We refused that deal and said we would move. Joe sent me out to look for a house I liked, and if he liked it, we would buy it.

We found a house in Lakeview near Lake Pontchartrain. We were there alone until 1959 when Barbara's husband died of a sudden heart attack. They were in Milwaukee so I took a plane and went after her and the children. For something to do she took a year at a business college and then went to Tulane to earn a teaching degree. She is still teaching. She had two small children when she came home – one a baby, so our being around was a help. In 1969 she remarried [to James Dearie, Jr.], and now lives in north Louisiana.

Steve came home from the Air Force after spending two years in Wyoming and two years in the middle of Australia. He went to LSUNO for about a year and then to Loyola Law School. He finished that and passed the bar exam. He is now a trial lawyer. He married [Paula] in 1967 and they have one son. They live here in New Orleans.

When Joe, Jr. got out of college, Goodyear offered him a job in their Aerospace Division. He is still there. He married [Julia] in 1964 and they have two sons. They live in Ohio.

Joe died of lung cancer in 1970, - a very much missed man.
Thelma T. Huber

Chapter 10

Thelma's Secrets

Even though we were close as a family, we have very recently discovered that our mother, Thelma, had some fascinating secrets.

Name

Perhaps the biggest one was her name, a secret she took to her grave, because we thought we knew what it was and never asked. To us she was always Thelma Belle Frances Thompson Huber.

I always enjoyed the fact that she had an extra middle name. Belle was the name of her grandmother, Belle Dyke, whose husband Samuel started the toy industry in Akron, allowing Akron to eventually become the toy capital of the world.

Recently the wife of a second cousin who is also, like Thelma's children, a great-grandchild of Samuel Comley Dyke, published the diary of her aunt by marriage (one of my mother's six cousins) *Thelma's Diary 1935*. From this we learned that among the six grandchildren of Samuel and Belle Dyke there were two Thelmas and another Frances, Ula Frances.

The Thelma Fern of *Thelma's Diary 1935* was a year younger than our mother, and the book covers her diary for the trip around the world that she took accompanied by a younger sister, Marjorie, in 1935. This was certainly very daring at that time for two unescorted young ladies in their twenties.

In researching whether there could be both two Thelmas and two named Frances, an attempt was made to obtain a copy of my mother's birth certificate. This failed as she was born too early for the local county recordkeeping. A certified copy of the birth register only gave her name as Thelma B.

A search of family records that survived Hurricane Katrina revealed only that on one bank account she went by Thelma Belle.

We have concluded that her name was certainly at least Thelma Belle Thompson Huber. Where and when the name Frances came from remains a mystery.

Fortune

Joyce Wiedie, who put her aunt's diary into context and wrote the surrounding material (and is listed as coauthor), ended her book with the "fortune" question. How did two young ladies of modest homes find the money for an expensive around-the-world cruise? Not only was it extensive, taking 192 days, but they also spent the money to take a side trip to visit our family on the Pathfinder Plantation in the fall of 1935.

That was our first year on the plantation, and our mother was in the process of refurbishing the approximately 13,000-square-foot house and training a staff of nine or ten. *Such a Life* does not mention this visit, which came as Thelma was expecting my sister who was born at the end of 1935.

My parents were extremely closemouthed about finances and details of their wonderful marriage. Thelma had said that she had inherited a few hundred dollars, and we assumed that this was sometime in the thirties. My father's brother, who handled our family's finances while my parents were overseas, did tell me of my mother's investment skills. In every case where they invested in common and preferred stocks in the same company, they chose differently and my mother always chose the best one.

Taking hints, I contacted the courthouse in the West Virginia county where Samuel C. Dyke died and I obtained copies of the will and probate filings. These not only identified the source of the money for Marjorie and Thelma Fern to go around the world, but they also explained other aspects of my mother's life. They shed light on certain family tensions and revealed why my great-aunts would not discuss certain things.

Samuel C. Dyke died in 1924, having outlived two wives. He left a short and unusual will. The key section IV reads:

> All of the residue of my estate, real, mixed and personal, wherever situate, I give bequeath and devise to my son Willis R. Dyke, and his children living at the time of my death: to my daughter Maude E. Breitenstein and her children living at the time of my death; to Grace I. Hays, my daughter, and her children living at the time of my death: and to Ethel Dyke, my daughter, and her children living at the time of death—should she marry and have children, per capita, share and share alike.

In *Such a Life* my mother states only that "since he and Grandmother were divorced, the money was divided amongst his four children and seven grandchildren." Actually, Belle Dyke died after the divorce, long before Samuel Dyke's demise, and his second wife also predeceased him.

A subsequent filing listed total assets of $101,068.38, equivalent in 2014 dollars to some 1.4 million dollars. After debts and expenses, there was, in 2014 dollars, over $550,000, or over $50,000 for each recipient. This clearly explains how two young women could afford to go around the world, particularly at a time when labor costs, taxes, and government-dictated expenses were much lower.

As usual, inherited money was a cause of friction in the family. The unmarried daughter, instead of receiving a fourth of the estate received only an eleventh. In dividing up the Dyke burial site, only two of the children and their spouses could be accommodated, not including the single daughter, nor Thelma's mother, Grace Irene Dyke Thompson Hays. Only the silverware was divided equally among the four children of Samuel C. Dyke.

Thus when our parents met, Thelma had a modest inheritance and he had a very promising job and was about to go to exotic climes. Moreover, he worked for a large, stable company known for a paternalistic attitude toward its employees. When did Dad learn that Thelma had some money? I am positive it was a bonus and not an incentive.

Both our parents were very careful with money, which permitted them to fund our educations and their end-of-life health costs and to leave a bit to help with educating their grandchildren.

It explains the separate apartment and the teenager hired to clean it when Thelma went to work for Goodyear, the Stutz Bearcat she drove in 1933, and her buying her mother and stepfather's house. Of course, Dad made a good income, and living on the plantation in company-supplied housing gave them the opportunity to save.

More fascinating perhaps is that my mother's story provided the background and probably the impetus for Thelma Fern and Marjorie's trip around the world. In 1928 in going to Sumatra my parents had gone partway around the globe. They completed the world circuit in 1932 on their return to Depression-era USA.

I feel certain that my mother's stories after her return to the USA in 1932 were an inspiration for Thelma Fern and Marjorie's desire to follow in their cousin's (my mother's) footsteps in 1935. And indeed, much of their trip did follow the same route. Their excursion to the plantation provided a haven to be with family.

Chapter 11

Postscript

In the years after Thelma's death in 1973, there would be one more granddaughter.

Thelma's son Stephen was a senior corporate councilor with Liberty Mutual until he retired, and he had a daughter after Thelma died. His son has two sons and a daughter.

Thelma's daughter Barbara retired from teaching in the inner city schools of New Orleans. With her second husband she bought her parents' home in the Lakeview district of New Orleans after Thelma passed away. It was destroyed by Hurricane Katrina, which wiped out much of the Lakeview district, and they moved to Baton Rouge. Barbara has four grandchildren, two girls and two boys, as well as three step-grandsons.

Thelma's son Joseph Jr.'s company, Goodyear Aircraft Corporation, became Goodyear Aerospace Corporation and was sold and resold. Thus he retired from Lockheed Martin. His wife and he incorporated a new company that did subcontract work for Lockheed Martin for eleven years. He and his wife have five grandsons.

As of 2014, Thelma has twelve great-grandchildren: nine boys and three girls.

References

1. Michael C. Cohill, *A Spin on the Past*. Hounding Productions, 2001. Michael has also drafted a separate biography of Samuel Dyke (beyond the brief one included in *A Spin on the Past*) which he has discussed with Joe Huber.

   Samuel Dyke is credited with starting the American industry in affordable manufactured toys and the first to sell directly to children. Per Cohill, "Thanks to Sam Dyke's inspiration, Akron became the birthplace of the modern American toy industry." By 1890 Dyke was producing a million clay marbles a day with his patented machines. By the end of the 1800s some twenty-four glass marble makers were operating in Akron, and the city well on its way to becoming the toy capital of the world. Cohill indicates that by 1929 there were over one hundred toy companies in operation within a thirty-mile radius of Akron.

   Samuel Dyke later became an industrial ambassador for the US president.

2. Thelma F. Dyke and Joyce M. Wiedie, *Thelma's Diary 1935*. AuthorHouse, 2013.

About the Author

Any autobiography of a son's mother includes much of his. He grew up on a remote Filipino rubber plantation, eighty miles from the nearest city and accessible only by water. Surrounded by servants in a huge house, he and his siblings each had their own *amah* (nanny) until he was six. Before he was eight, he had crossed the Pacific Ocean three times on luxury liners in month-long voyages.

Then came thirty-one months of imprisonment. He was proud of his contribution to the family's efforts during their time in Japanese prison camps when he was a young boy.

After their family was saved from death by starvation in the largest rescue of allied civilians in WWII, he went back to the Philippines for an idyllic few years before returning to America for high school.

Following an education in electrical engineering at MIT, he found love and helped raise a family that includes two sons, their lovely wives, and five grandsons. He and his wife have had fifty wonderful years together so far.

He has traveled over much of the world on business, taking his family for months to Greece and weeks in Great Britain and elsewhere in Europe. He devoted his career to repaying America for the family's rescue. His inventions, equipment designs and work supported the Cold War, the War on Drugs, and the War on Terror.

He continues to be active in his church and a number of organizations and spends his free time with his passions for history, archeology, and books.